Chords, Riffs & Effects
you can learn today!

FastForward™

Funk
Guitar

with Rikky Rooksby

FastForward™

Chords, Riffs & Effects you can learn today!

Funk Guitar

with Rikky Rooksby

Wise Publications
London / New York / Sydney / Paris / Copenhagen / Madrid / Tokyo

Exclusive Distributors:
Music Sales Limited
8/9 Frith Street, London W1D 3JB, England.
Music Sales Pty Limited
120 Rothschild Avenue, Rosebery, NSW 2018, Australia.
Music Sales Corporation
257 Park Avenue South, New York, NY10010,
United States of America.

Order No. AM958529
ISBN 0-7119-8222-8
This book © Copyright 2001 by Wise Publications.

Written and arranged by Rikky Rooksby.
Edited by Sorcha Armstrong.
Music processed by Paul Ewers Music Design.
Cover Photograph (1995 Fender 'Moto' Stratocaster
limited edition in plastic pearl finish)
courtesy of Outline Press.
Text photographs courtesy of
London Features International, Redferns & Retna.

Printed and bound in the United Kingdom.

Your Guarantee of Quality:
As publishers, we strive to produce every book to
the highest commercial standards.
The music has been freshly engraved and the book has
been carefully designed to minimise awkward page turns
and to make playing from it a real pleasure.
Particular care has been given to specifying acid-free,
neutral-sized paper made from pulps which have not
been elemental chlorine bleached.
This pulp is from farmed sustainable forests and
was produced with special regard for the environment.
Throughout, the printing and binding have
been planned to ensure a sturdy, attractive publication
which should give years of enjoyment.
If your copy fails to meet our high standards, please
inform us and we will gladly replace it.

Music Sales' complete catalogue describes
thousands of titles and is available in full colour sections
by subject, direct from Music Sales Limited.
Please state your areas of interest and send a cheque/postal
order for £1.50 for postage to: Music Sales Limited,
Newmarket Road, Bury St. Edmunds, Suffolk IP33 3YB.

www.musicsales.com

Guitar Tablature Explained

Guitar music can be notated three different ways: on a musical stave, in tablature, and in rhythm slashes

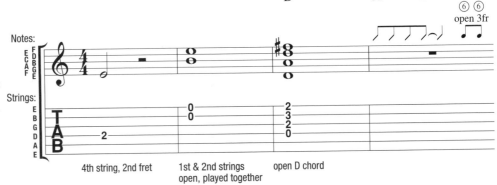

RHYTHM SLASHES are written above the stave. Strum chords in the rhythm indicated. Round noteheads indicate single notes.

THE MUSICAL STAVE shows pitches and rhythms and is divided by lines into bars. Pitches are named after the first seven letters of the alphabet.

TABLATURE graphically represents the guitar fingerboard. Each horizontal line represents a string, and each number represents a fret.

4th string, 2nd fret   1st & 2nd strings open, played together   open D chord

definitions for special guitar notation

SEMI-TONE BEND: Strike the note and bend up a semi-tone (1/2 step).

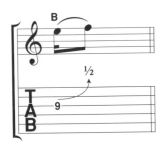

WHOLE-TONE BEND: Strike the note and bend up a whole-tone (whole step).

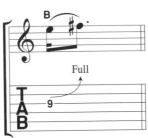

GRACE NOTE BEND: Strike the note and bend as indicated. Play the first note as quickly as possible.

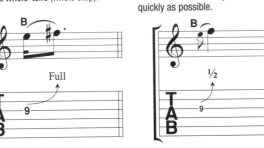

QUARTER-TONE BEND: Strike the note and bend up a 1/4 step.

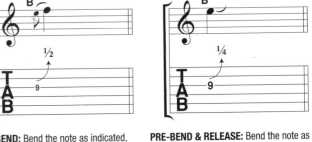

BEND & RELEASE: Strike the note and bend up as indicated, then release back to the original note.

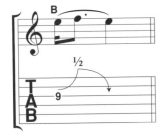

COMPOUND BEND & RELEASE: Strike the note and bend up and down in the rhythm indicated.

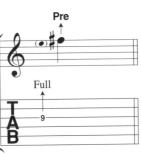

PRE-BEND: Bend the note as indicated, then strike it.

PRE-BEND & RELEASE: Bend the note as indicated. Strike it and release the note back to the original pitch.

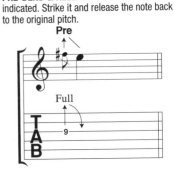

UNISON BEND: Strike the two notes simultaneously and bend the lower note up to the pitch of the higher.

BEND & RESTRIKE: Strike the note and bend as indicated then restrike the string where the symbol occurs.

BEND, HOLD AND RELEASE: Same as bend and release but hold the bend for the duration of the tie.

BEND AND TAP: Bend the note as indicated and tap the higher fret while still holding the bend.

VIBRATO: The string is vibrated by rapidly bending and releasing the note with the fretting hand.

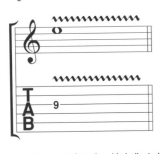

HAMMER-ON: Strike the first (lower) note with one finger, then sound the higher note (on the same string) with another finger by fretting it without picking.

PULL-OFF: Place both fingers on the notes to be sounded, Strike the first note and without picking, pull the finger off to sound the second (lower) note.

LEGATO SLIDE (GLISS): Strike the first note and then slide the same fret-hand finger up or down to the second note. The second note is not struck.

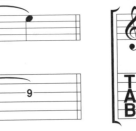

NOTE: The speed of any bend is indicated by the music notation and tempo.

SHIFT SLIDE (GLISS & RESTRIKE): Same as legato slide, except the second note is struck.

TRILL: Very rapidly alternate between the notes indicated by continuously hammering on and pulling off.

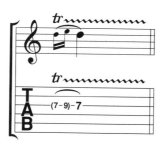

TAPPING: Hammer ("tap") the fret indicated with the pick-hand index or middle finger and pull off to the note fretted by the fret hand.

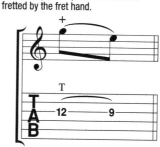

PICK SCRAPE: The edge of the pick is rubbed down (or up) the string, producing a scratchy sound.

MUFFLED STRINGS: A percussive sound is produced by laying the fret hand across the string(s) without depressing, and striking them with the pick hand.

NATURAL HARMONIC: Strike the note while the fret-hand lightly touches the string directly over the fret indicated.

PINCH HARMONIC: The note is fretted normally and a harmonic is produced by adding the edge of the thumb or the tip of the index finger of the pick hand to the normal pick attack.

HARP HARMONIC: The note is fretted normally and a harmonic is produced by gently resting the pick hand's index finger directly above the indicated fret (in parentheses) while the pick hand's thumb or pick assists by plucking the appropriate string.

PALM MUTING: The note is partially muted by the pick hand lightly touching the string(s) just before the bridge.

RAKE: Drag the pick across the strings indicated with a single motion.

TREMOLO PICKING: The note is picked as rapidly and continuously as possible.

ARPEGGIATE: Play the notes of the chord indicated by quickly rolling them from bottom to top.

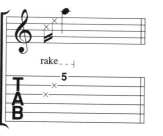

SWEEP PICKING: Rhythmic downstroke and/or upstroke motion across the strings.

VIBRATO DIVE BAR AND RETURN: The pitch of the note or chord is dropped a specific number of steps (in rhythm) then returned to the original pitch.

VIBRATO BAR SCOOP: Depress the bar just before striking the note, then quickly release the bar.

VIBRATO BAR DIP: Strike the note and then immediately drop a specific number of steps, then release back to the original pitch.

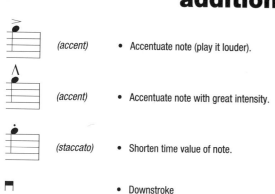
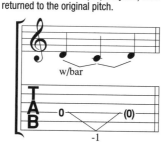

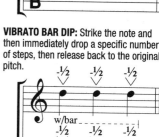

additional musical definitions

 (accent)	• Accentuate note (play it louder).	
∧ (accent)	• Accentuate note with great intensity.	
(staccato)	• Shorten time value of note.	
⊓	• Downstroke	
V	• Upstroke	

D.%. al Coda

• Go back to the sign (%), then play until the bar marked *To Coda ⊕* then skip to the section marked *⊕ Coda.*

D.C. al Fine

• Go back to the beginning of the song and play until the bar marked *Fine* (end).

tacet

• Instrument is silent (drops out).

• Repeat bars between signs.

1. **2.**

• When a repeated section has different endings, play the first ending only the first time and the second ending only the second time.

Introduction

Hello, and welcome to ▶▶**Fast***Forward*.

Congratulations on purchasing a product that will improve your playing and provide you with hours of pleasure. All the music in this book has been specially created by professional musicians to give you maximum value and enjoyment.

If you already know how to 'drive' your instrument, but you'd like to do a little customising, you've pulled in at the right place. We'll put you on the fast track to playing the kinds of riffs and patterns that today's professionals rely on.

We'll provide you with a vocabulary of riffs that you can apply in a wide variety of musical situations, with a special emphasis on giving you the techniques that will help you in a band situation.

▶▶**Fast***Forward* *Funk Guitar* will introduce you to the language of Funk, and what creates its distinctive sound. You'll learn the essential chords, riffs, intros and fills that are used by classic soul and funk bands, such as **Kool & The Gang**, **James Brown**, and **Funkadelic**.

Learn the secrets of 16th-note strumming, how to use Wah-Wah, and the most important element of funk – the rhythms that make the funk sound. In no time, you'll be amazing your friends and family, and making the staff in your local guitar shop green with envy!

Each example in this book is given in musical score, guitar tablature (TAB), and has a corresponding CD track. If you're not too familiar with TAB, it's pretty simple: each number indicates the fret at which the note is played, and each line is a string, going from low to high, i.e. the lowest line on the TAB corresponds to the lowest string on your guitar.

If you find it hard to remember which way up they go, think always of pitch: high notes are above low notes, therefore the highest-sounding string (E) is at the top. Other TAB symbols will be explained as we go along, and there's also a handy reference guide to the most common of these, on pages 6 and 7.

Each musical example is played once with your guitar part, and once without. The first is for you to learn by listening, the second 'play-along' track is for you to practise.

The examples have a one-bar count-in.

TRACK 1 tuning notes

Tip

Use the tuning notes supplied on Track 1 to tune your guitar to our CD. The first note is the bottom E string, continuing with A, D, G, B and finally top E.

Funk Guitar

Funk and soul guitar is an integral part of the music of such varied artists as **Parliament, Earth Wind & Fire, Bootsy Collins, Sly & the Family Stone, The Average White Band, Funkadelic, The Meters, Fatback Band, The Commodores, George Clinton, Osibisa, KC & the Sunshine Band, The Gap Band, Kool & the Gang, James Brown**, and **The Ohio Players.**

It's a style that has influenced '90s bands like the **Red Hot Chili Peppers** and many dance and rock acts. As for the names... well, guitarists like **Jimmy Nolan (James Brown), Prince, Nile Rodgers (Chic), Melvin 'Wah-Wah' Watson, Denis Coffey, Robert White, Joe Messina, Eddie Willis** and **Marv Tarplin** (Motown), **Steve Cropper (Booker T. & the MG's), Phil Upchurch, Eddie Hazel (Funkadelic), Ernie Isley (Isley Brothers)**, and **Curtis Mayfield**... to name just a few!

▶▶**Fast***Forward* *Funk Guitar* looks at many techniques which have characterised funk, soul and R'n'B guitar playing. The essence of funk and soul guitar is rhythm. These strains of black music are bound up with the dancefloor and the bands who have recorded in these styles are among the tightest rhythm sections ever to magnetise tape.

Funk guitar may not look as obviously virtuoso as, say, rock lead but it often depends on what could be termed 'hidden musicianship' to play these styles. It takes skill to lock into a drum/bass groove and stay right in time, right on the money.

▶▶**Fast***Forward* *Funk Guitar* introduces you to funk and soul guitar rhythms, important chords like the dominant 9th and the minor 7th, four-string chord shapes, abbreviated 11th and 13ths, chromatic runs, syncopation, unison bass and guitar riffs, the importance of rests and the downbeat, and 16th note strumming. If you are used to playing rock or blues guitar it will change the way you feel rhythm and inspire you to play in a manner that will make people ask, 'How do you get that sound?'.

All players and bands get their sounds and styles by drawing on the same basic building blocks. With ▶▶**Fast***Forward* you'll quickly learn these, and then be ready to use them to create your own style.

1: Single Note Funk

Single Note Riff

Let's start nice and easy with a typical two-chord change over which we'll play a simple single note riff. Like rock music, funk is often built on repeated short riffs – musical figures played again and again. Sometimes they're pitched in the guitar's mid-range, other times lower. If they're lower they often share the notes with the bass guitar. This generates the powerful 'bottom-end' that makes funk and other soul styles so... well... funkadelic!

Don't be concerned about the apparent complexity of the conventional music notation. Written down, funk and soul rhythms can be quite complicated. This is because they make frequent use of 16th (semi-quaver) notes, 16th note rests, ties and syncopation – the latter meaning where the notes do not necessarily fall

on the beat. This is what makes the music groove. But your ears will soon adjust to the rhythm as you listen to the examples on the backing tracks. The conventional notation can then be a guide. Use your ears first to feel your way into the rhythm.

The notes used in 'Chester's Weekend' are taken from the scale of G pentatonic minor (G B♭ C D F), a popular scale in funk and soul, as it is in rock and blues. It has a characteristically 'tough' sound. The term 'pentatonic' simply means a five note scale.

To get the effect of the rests – where there is no note – release the pressure of the fretting finger against the fretboard once you have played a note such as the first G in bar 1 or the first C in bar 2.

 **TRACKS 2+3**

Chester's Weekend

Chromatic Patterns

By the way, you may be wondering 'Who is Chester?' Just imagine that the examples in ▶▶**Fast Forward** *Funk Guitar* are taken from the soundtrack of a film called *Hustler's Midnight*, starring detective and general cool dude Chester Monro. Keep a box of popcorn handy and let the titles suggest the story as we go along...

'Stake-out On 39th' uses the same scale but in the middle register of the guitar. Watch out for the 'double-stops' in bars 6 and 7. A double-stop is where you hold down two notes at the same time. Notice how these thicken the riff. These are the kind of notes you might find in a **Chuck Berry**-inspired rock'n'roll guitar solo, yet because of the musical context they sound different.

Watch out for the extra chromatic notes in the last bar. Chromatic means notes that don't belong to the main scale of the music. So B♮ and C♯ are chromatic in the scale of G pentatonic minor (G B♭ C D F).

There are three tracks on the CD for this example. Track 4 demonstrates just the written notes – so when you see a rest, don't play.

Track 5 does something a bit different. Where you see a rest, a muted strum is played, in 16th notes. Listen carefully to both versions to get the feel of this idea.

Track 6 is the backing track for both versions.

The 16th Note Strum

The 16th note strum is a vital part of funk guitar. It means strumming four times – down, up, down, up – on each beat. You have to keep the wrist of your strumming hand nice and relaxed.

When there is no note marked on the stave you need to be careful to dampen, or mute, all the strings while the strumming hand carries on hitting them. This creates a distinctive rhythmic effect – a 'clicking' sound in between the notes.

Don't worry about getting all the 16th strums in – it's the effect that counts. No listener will be counting all 16 strums in a bar and then tell you you missed one! They'll be too busy 'getting down'!

There will be later examples of 16th note strumming in the book. Feel free to experiment playing any of the examples in this manner as well as playing them 'straight' with just the written notes sounding.

TRACKS 4+5+6

Stake-out On 39th

Pentatonic Riff

'Ball Of Confucius' is another pentatonic riff, this time in D (D F G A C) with one chromatic note added, the C♯ in bar 1. Notice how when the chord changes to G in bar 4 the riff is moved (transposed) up to start on G.

Watch out for the 16th notes in bar 10 and make sure the last few notes are rhythmically tight. The underlying feel of the chord sequence is similar to a 12-bar pattern.

Ball Of Confucius

G Mixolydian

Chester is after his man in 'The Pursuit', a typically slinky off-beat ascending riff using a scale known as G mixolydian. This is simply G major (G A B C D E F♯) with F♮ instead of F♯ (though you'll find both in this piece).

The major notes give a more upbeat tone to the music compared with the pentatonic minor we've used so far. From bar 5 onward notice that an extra note (C♯) is squeezed into the riff. As with many funk riffs, this ends with a twist in the tail: a bunch of 16th notes.

TRACKS 9+10

The Pursuit

Theme From Hustler's Midnight

Roll the credits, here's 'Theme from Hustler's Midnight'. It has a two-bar intro before settling down to a G pentatonic minor riff higher than the previous ones you've played. When the chord changes to C7 the guitar part plays some sliding and bent notes, half-way between a riff and a solo.

Listen for the bars in this piece where you are playing a single note several times in succession with rests in between as a rhythmic motif. In funk music such a figure might well be doubled by keyboards or brass or bass... or all of them!

Theme From Hustler's Midnight

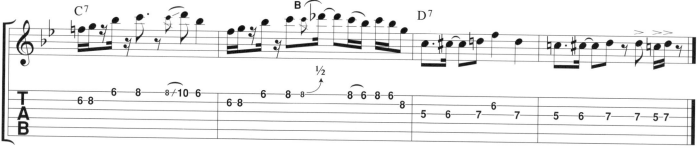

Octave Figures

In funk and disco one of the most important musical figures is the octave. 'Down the Alley' features a riff built largely on an octave leap from G to G before introducing consecutive octaves to fatten the sound in bars 4, 5 and 7. The trick with playing octaves is to damp strings that fall between the notes you are striking.

Compare the notes on the first beat of bars 1, 2 and 3. Bar 1 starts with two evenly spaced 8th notes (quavers). In bar 2, these are replaced by four 16th notes (semi-quavers), also evenly

spaced. In bar 3 we find instead a dotted 8th note followed by a 16th. These two notes are not evenly spaced; the first lasts longer than the second. Listen carefully to the CD at that point and you will hear the 'spring' to the rhythm this gives. Funk and soul music is full of such 'dotted-note' rhythms.

Watch out for another one of those slinky chromatic sequences in bars 5-6, where the part moves from A to C via B♭ and B, one semi-tone at a time.

TRACKS 13+14

Down The Alley

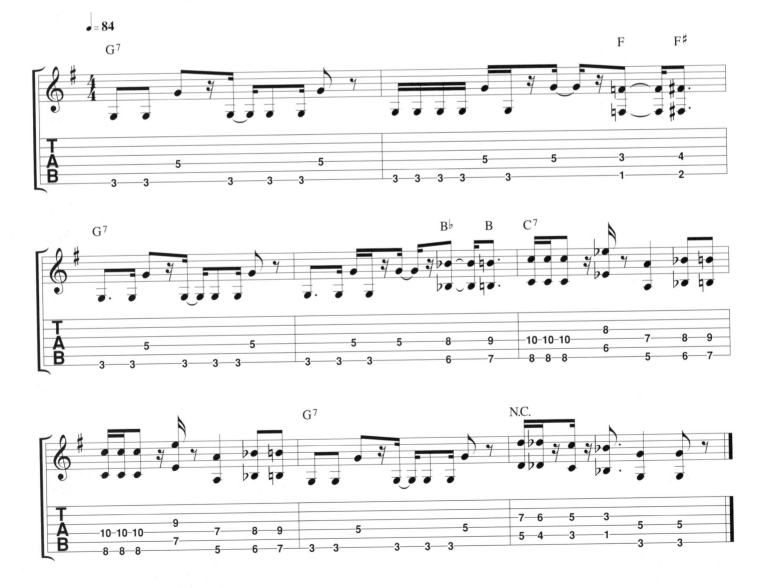

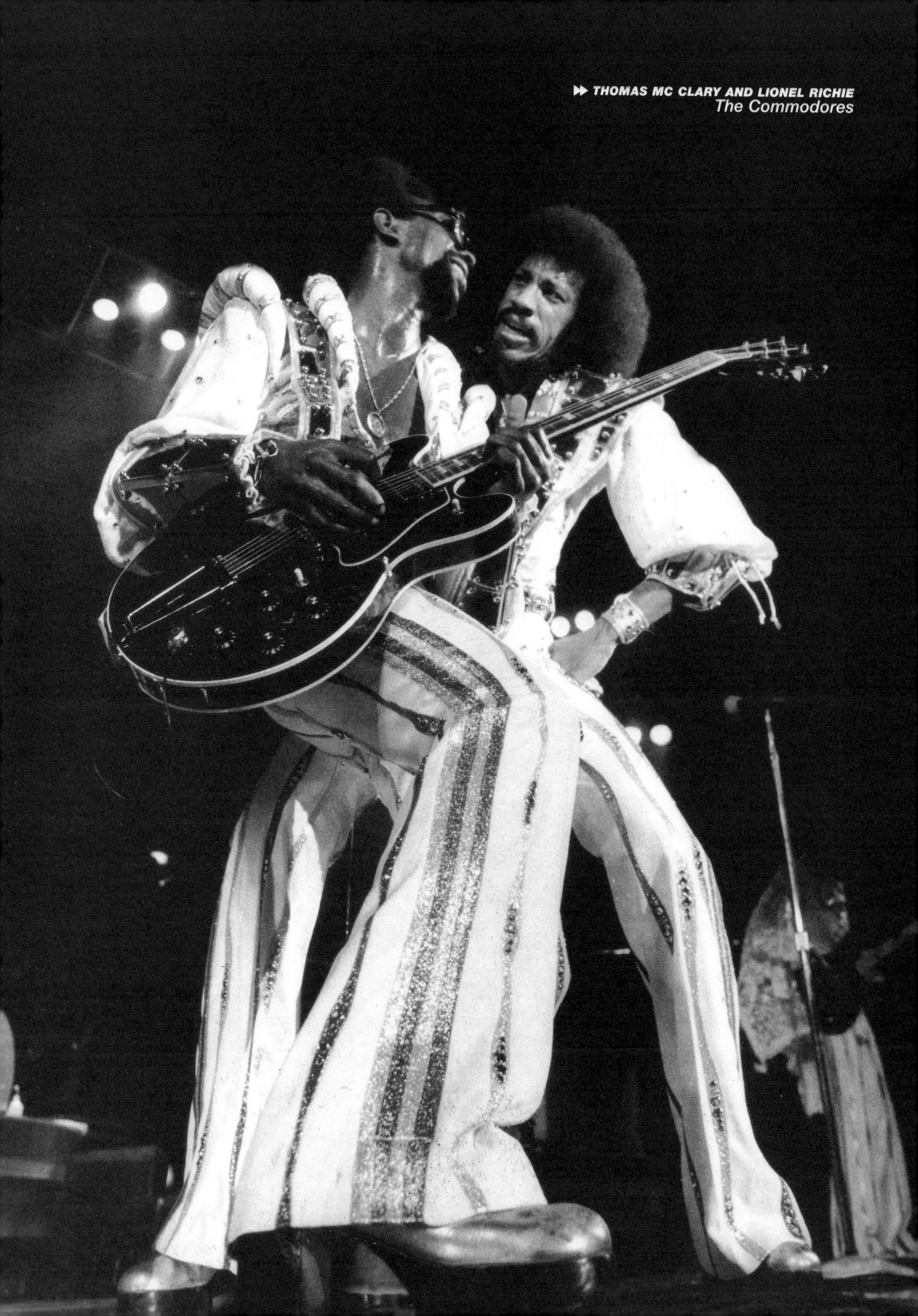

▶▶ THOMAS MC CLARY AND LIONEL RICHIE
The Commodores

Using Wah-Wah

In the late 1960s the wah-wah pedal became not only a favourite tool of rock players but also some soul guitarists. You can hear it on **Supremes** tracks, such as 'Up The Ladder To The Roof', and of course on the famous 'Shaft' soundtrack by **Isaac Hayes**.

'Dead End' uses octaves and continuous 16th note damped strumming. Bring the pedal slowly back and forth across the mid-point where it most obviously messes with the frequencies. If you don't have a wah-wah yet, don't worry... just wear a leather coat and a black sweater instead...

TRACKS 15+16

Dead End

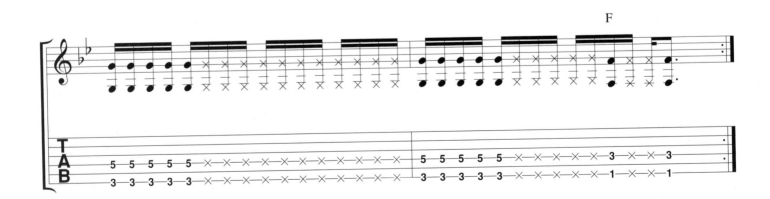

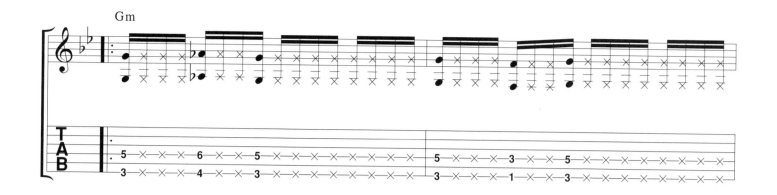

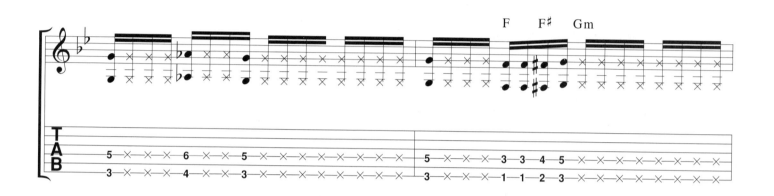

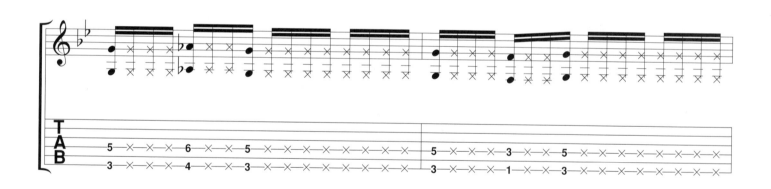

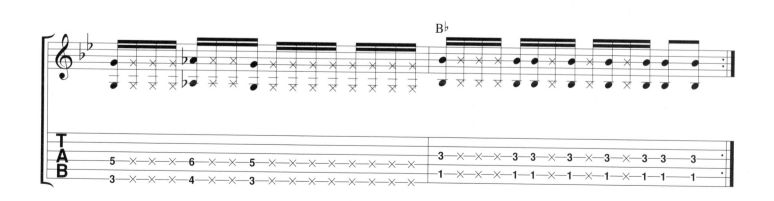

Rests

In 'Let the Cops Go Figure' we combine the octave leap idea with the double-stops that you played in 'Stake-out On 39th' and the rhythmically accented chromatic notes. Rests play a big part in bringing out the punch of the riff, especially in bars 4 and 8 where the B-C-D and B-C-C♯-D parts come in.

You will also find an E♭ dominant 9 chord in bar 2. This type of chord is very important to funk and soul guitar. We will look at it in more detail later, but for now, notice the dramatic effect of using this chord here. Later in the book you will learn how to combine single notes and chords in one piece.

TRACKS 17+18

Let The Cops Go Figure

▶▶ **GEORGE CLINTON**
Parliament/ Funkadelic

2: A Mini Funk Chord Dictionary

Funk and soul chords

Here are some of the most useful chords for playing soul and funk guitar. Many of them only use the top four strings. That's because bands that play this type of music often have more members than the average power-trio or quartet of Rock and Blues. This means the guitar has to share more sonic space. It has to 'sit' – to find a niche – amid other instruments like keyboards, brass and the rhythm section.

Partial Chords

With other instruments covering the low-end, five or six string chords are not always necessary. It's the top four strings of the guitar that will cut through.

9th, 11th and 13th chords

The use of 9th, 11th and 13th chords also means that a guitarist needs to abbreviate them into more manageable and effective forms. A complete 11th chord actually requires six different notes, and a complete 13th seven notes – which since most guitars only have six strings is a little tricky! That's why in practice, 11th and 13th chords played on guitar tend to be found in these kind of shortened forms.

Moveable Shapes

The Mini Funk Chord Dictionary contains moveable chord shapes for some of the most common funk chords. If you check which string has the root note (1) you will be able to move these up and down the neck to get the right pitch for whatever you are playing.

For example, chord box six is a minor chord with its root on the B string. This makes a chord of D minor, as it's printed here. So if you wanted to play F#m in this shape, you would simply have to move the whole shape up, until the second string note becomes F# (at the 7th fret).

Minor 7/ Major 6

Notice the minor 7 which is also marked as a major 6 (chord box 14). This means it can be used as either, depending on the root note. If you use it as a minor 7, the root note is on the top string. In this example, it makes a chord of Fm7. If you want to use it as a major 6 chord, treat the note on the third string as the root. Here, this would be A♭, so the shape could be used as an A♭6.

Dominant 7

Don't worry about the theory of how the dominant 7 or 9 get their name. Just remember that the dominant 7 (A7, B7, D7 etc) is the tough, bluesy sounding chord, and the major 7 chord (Amaj7, Dmaj7, etc) has a smoother, more romantic sound. The minor 7 doesn't sound as sad as a straight minor and combines nicely with the major 7.

Dominant 9

There are three shapes for the dominant 9 chord, which is very important in funk and soul. You played one in track 7 and you will be using it more soon. The dominant 9 can be played where you might use a dominant 7, as long as the root is the same. They are closely related chords.

Mini Funk Chord Dictionary

major

1 3 5 1

major

5 1 3 5

major

3 5 1 3

minor

1 ♭3 5 1

minor

5 1 ♭3 5

minor

♭3 5 1 ♭3

dom7

5 1 3 ♭7

dom7

5 ♭7 3

dom7

1　♭7 3 5

maj7

5 1 3 7

maj7

1 5 7 3

min7

5 1 ♭3 ♭7

min7

5 1 ♭7 ♭3

min7/maj6

♭7 ♭3 5 1
(or) 5 1 3 6

min7

1　♭7 ♭3 5

min7

1 5 ♭7 ♭3 1 5
(♭7)

dom7sus4

1 5 ♭7 4 5

7♯5

♭7 3 ♯5 1

7♯9

1 3 ♭7 ♯9

dom9

1 3 ♭7 9 5

dim9

1 3 ♭7 9

min9

♭7 ♭3 ♭7 9

11

♭7 3 11 9

13

♭7 3 13 9

min13

♭7 ♭3 13 9

Example 1

Now it's time to return to 16th note strumming. At this point we're going to do some exercises which are designed to help your strumming hand. Example 1 requires you to hold down a C♯m7 chord at the 4th fret. Your strumming hand will be hitting the strings four times on each beat – down, up, down, up. At first you sound the chord on the first beat of a bar, then beats 1 and 3, then each of the four beats, and finally the rhythm becomes more developed. Squeeze the chord onto the fretboard whenever it needs to sound and then relax the barre when it doesn't – but don't let go of the chord shape. You should be holding it against the strings so as to damp, or mute, them – but don't press it against the fretboard except on the beats where it is meant to sound. The percussion on the track should help you nail the rhythm.

= chord damped

= chord sounded

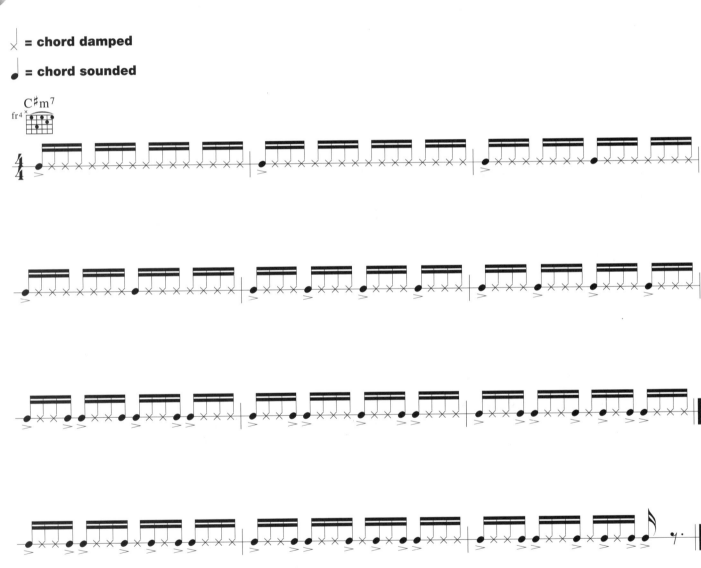

Example 2

Example 2 uses a similar approach with C♯m7, F♯m7 and G♯m7 chords.

= chord damped

= chord sounded

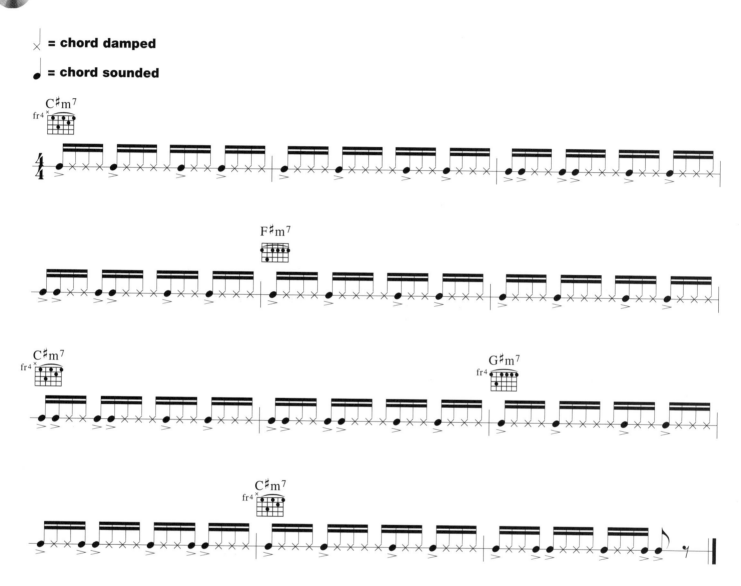

Example 3

Here, we have some dominant 9 chords in five and
four string versions in a 12-bar sequence.

TRACKS 23+24

𝄾 = chord damped

♩ = chord sounded

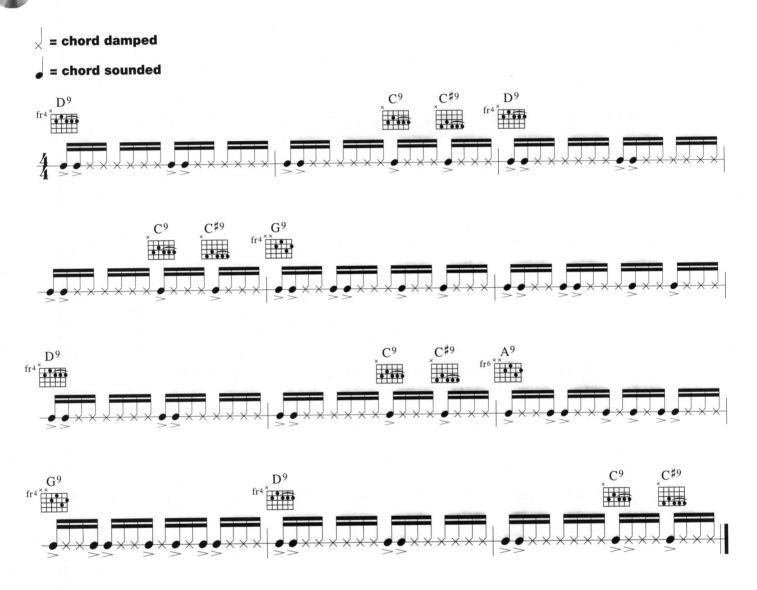

3: Using Funk Chords

In this section we are going to play around with some chordal ideas. 'Hustler's Shuffle' takes a simple three-note chord and does something unusual with it. If you look at the chord in bar 1 you will see that it is written as a dominant 7 shape. However, because of the B bass note that triad is instead heard as a minor 6.

This shows that in funk playing you may not always play the root note yourself – it might be your bass player. So even if you're a bit worried about those platform boots and strange star-shaped specs he wears, you may need to check things out with him from time to time!

TRACKS 25+26

Hustler's Shuffle

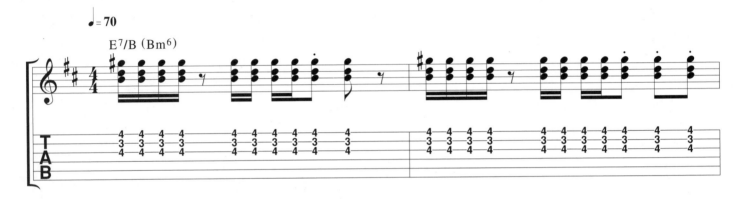

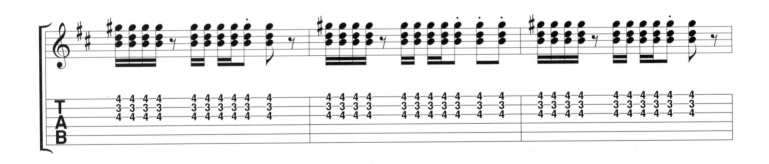

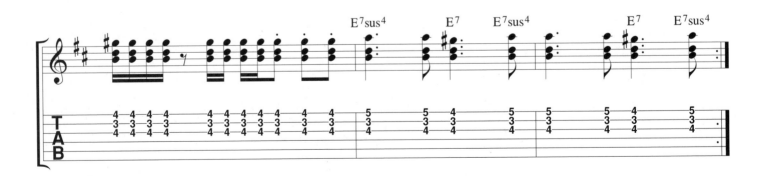

Off-beat Triads

'Dance Scene' has a definite uptempo **Earth, Wind and Fire** feel. It's simply made up of triads played on the off-beat. Watch out for bars 4 and 8, with the F#7sus4 and the F# aug chords.

Dance Scene

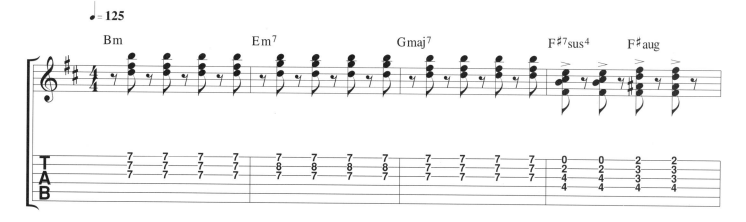

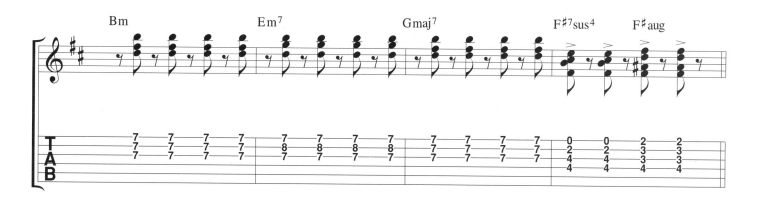

On The Upbeat

'Dance Scene, Fancy Moves' illustrates how you
can take a slightly different approach to the same
chord sequence. A song might well have both
this guitar part and the previous going at the
same time. This part is made up of fourths (bar
1) and thirds (bar 4). Notice how the guitar
avoids the strong downbeats.

TRACKS 29+30

Dance Scene, Fancy Moves

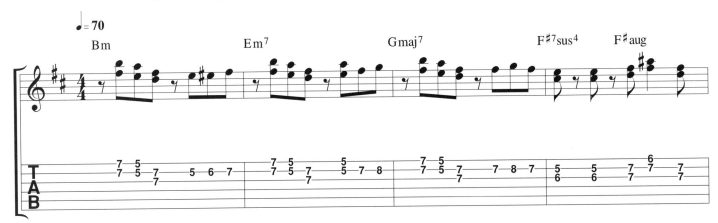

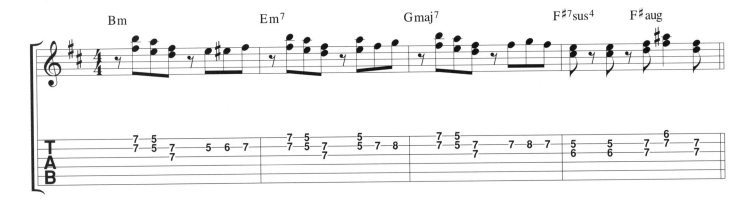

▶▶ FastForward™
Guide To Guitar

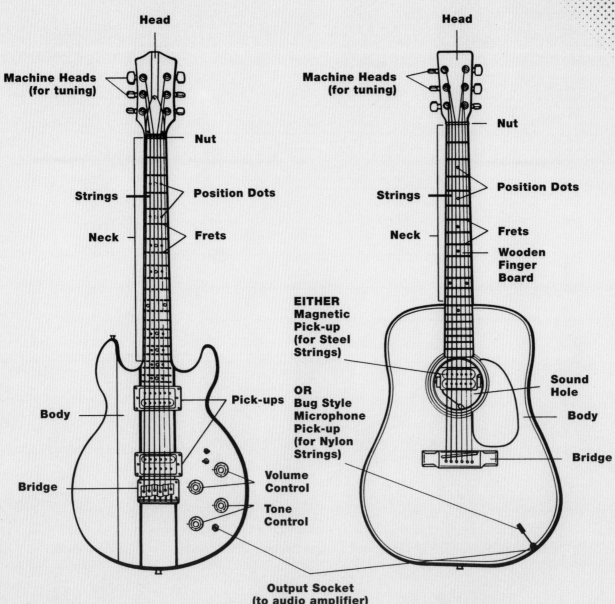

Head

Machine Heads
(for tuning)

Nut

Strings

Position Dots

Neck

Frets

Body

Pick-ups

Bridge

Volume
Control

Tone
Control

EITHER
Magnetic
Pick-up
(for Steel
Strings)

OR
Bug Style
Microphone
Pick-up
(for Nylon
Strings)

Output Socket
(to audio amplifier)

Head

Machine Heads
(for tuning)

Nut

Strings

Position Dots

Neck

Frets

Wooden
Finger
Board

Sound
Hole

Body

Bridge

The Guitar

Whether you have an acoustic or an electric guitar, the principles of playing are fundamentally the same, and so are most of the features on both instruments.

In order to 'electrify' an acoustic guitar (as in the diagram), a magnetic pick up can be attached to those guitars with steel strings or a 'bug' style microphone pick-up can be attached to guitars with nylon strings.

If in doubt check with your local music shop.

Tuning Your Guitar

Tuning
Accurate tuning of the guitar is essential, and is achieved by winding the machine heads up or down. It is always better to 'tune up' to the correct pitch rather than down.

Therefore, if you find that the pitch of your string is higher (sharper) than the correct pitch, you should 'wind down' below the correct pitch, and then 'tune up' to it.

Relative Tuning
Tuning the guitar to itself without the aid of a pitch pipe or other tuning device.

Other Methods Of Tuning
Pitch pipe
Tuning fork
Dedicated electronic guitar tuner

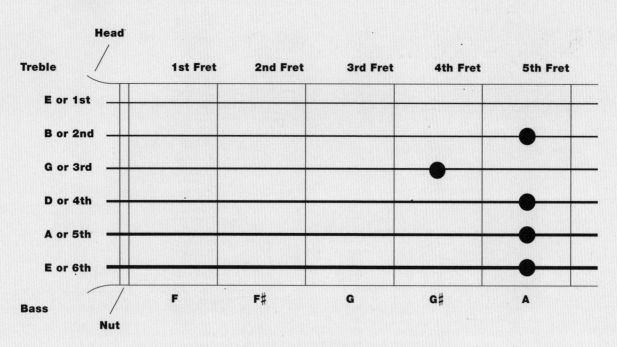

Press down where indicated, one at a time, following the instructions below.

Estimate the pitch of the 6th string as near as possible to **E** or at least a comfortable pitch (not too high or you might break other strings in tuning up).

Then, while checking the various positions on the above diagram, place a finger from your left hand on:

- The 5th fret of the E or 6th string and **tune the open A** (or 5th string) to the note (A)

- The 5th fret of the A or 5th string and **tune the open D** (or 4th string) to the note (D)

- The 5th fret of the D or 4th string and **tune the open G** (or 3rd string) to the note (G)

- The 4th fret of the G or 3rd string and **tune the open B** (or 2nd string) to the note (B)

- The 5th fret of the B or 2nd string and **tune the open E** (or 1st string) to the note (E)

Chord Boxes

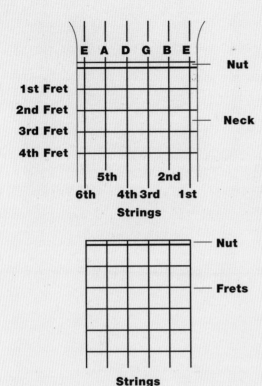

E A D G B E

Nut
1st Fret
2nd Fret
Neck
3rd Fret
4th Fret

5th   2nd
6th 4th 3rd 1st
Strings

Nut
Frets
Strings

The A Chord

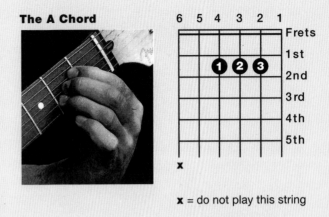

6 5 4 3 2 1

Frets
1st
① ② ③
2nd
3rd
4th
5th

x

x = do not play this string

Chord boxes are diagrams of the guitar neck viewed head upwards, face on, as illustrated in the above drawings. The horizontal double line at the top is the nut, the other horizontal lines are the frets. The vertical lines are the strings starting from E or 6th on the left to E or 1st on the right.

Any dots with numbers inside them simply indicate which finger goes where. Any strings marked with an **x** must not be played.

The fingers of your hand are numbered 1, 2, 3, & 4 as in the diagram below.

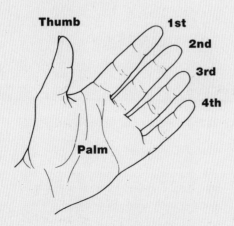

Thumb   1st
               2nd
               3rd
               4th
Palm

All chords are major chords unless otherwise indicated.

Left Hand
Place all three fingers into position and press down firmly. Keep your thumb around the middle of the back of the neck and directly behind your 1st and 2nd fingers.

Right Hand Thumb Or Plectrum
Slowly play each string, starting with the 5th or A string and moving up to the 1st or E string.

If there is any buzzing, perhaps you need to:-
Position your fingers nearer the metal fret (towards you); or adjust the angle of your hand; or check that the buzz is not elsewhere on the guitar by playing the open strings in the same manner.

Finally, your nails may be too long, in which case you are pressing down at an extreme angle and therefore not firmly enough. Also the pad of one of your fingers may be in the way of the next string for the same reason.

So, cut your nails to a more comfortable length and then try to keep them as near vertical to the fretboard as possible.

Once you have a 'buzz-free' sound, play the chord a few times and then remove your fingers and repeat the exercise until your positioning is right instinctively.

Hoiding The Guitar

Keep your thumb slightly to the left of your fingers which should be above the three treble strings as shown.

The picture above shows a comfortable position for playing rock or pop guitar

The Right Hand
When STRUMMING (brushing your fingers across the strings), hold your fingers together.

The Plectrum
Many modern guitar players prefer to use a plectrum to strike the strings. Plectrums come in many sizes, shapes and thicknesses and are available from your local music shop.

Start with a fairly large, soft one if possible, with a grip. The photo shows the correct way to hold your plectrum.

When PICKING (plucking strings individually), hold your wrist further away from the strings than for strumming.

The Left Hand
Use your fingertips to press down on the strings in the positions described. Your thumb should be behind your 1st and 2nd fingers pressing on the middle of the back of the neck.

▶▶ *JOHNNY GRAHM*
Earth, Wind & Fire

Major or Minor?

'Chester's Funk' is a 12-bar sequence where the bars use different chord forms on the same root note. In bar 1 we have a D7, D6 and Dm7, and likewise in bar 5 a G7, G6 and Gm7. It is quite common in funk to have this slight ambiguity about whether the music is major or minor.

Listen out for the 'jazzy' effect of the add13s and the A to B♭ semi-tone shift in the last couple of bars.

 **TRACKS 31+32**

Chester's Funk

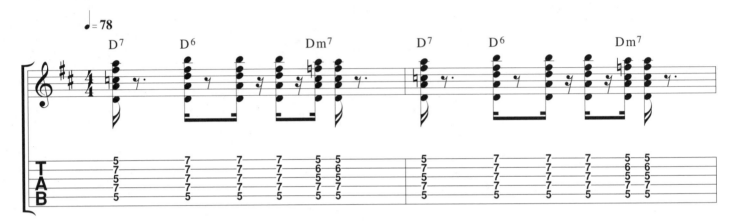

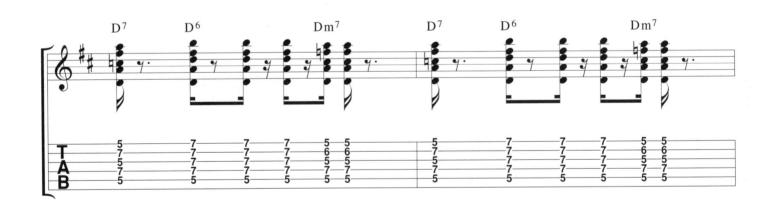

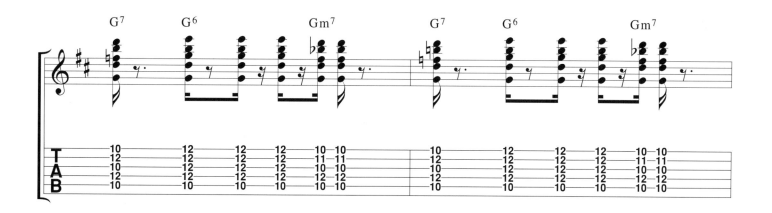

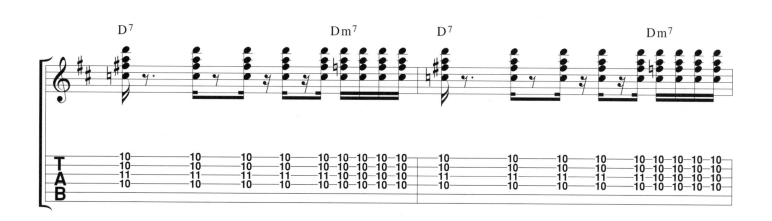

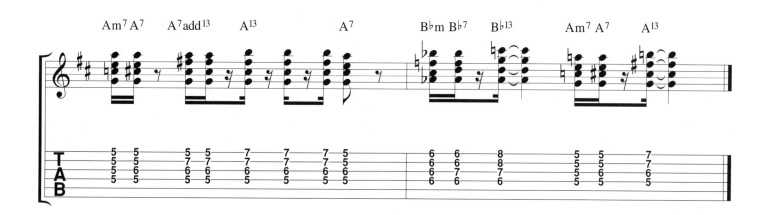

Semi-tone Shifts

Here's another typical feature of the funk sound –
semi-tone shifts of chords played with a strong
rhythm. This is especially true with the dominant
9 chord. 'You Gotta Be Kidding' is an opportunity
to do some yourself.

Enjoy the accented G9 when it comes in!

▶▶ AVERAGE WHITE BAND

You Gotta Be Kidding

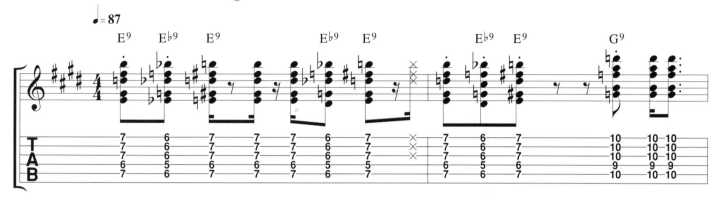

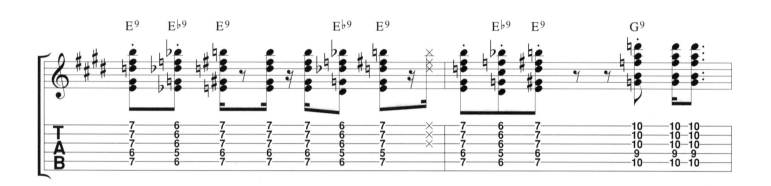

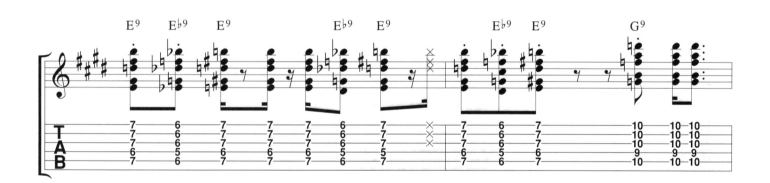

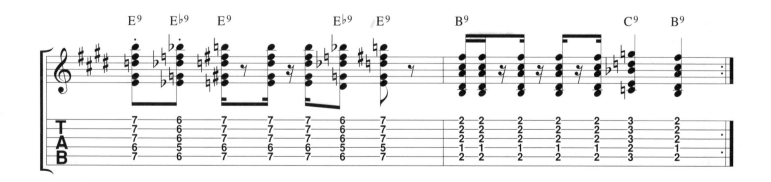

16th-note Strumming

'Hustler's Funk' continues in this vein, with a steadily developing rhythm that starts off with just a couple of strikes and then gets fuller as it goes along. Squeeze those chords on and off as and when you need them. You can try continuous 16th note damped strumming when you get more confident with the chord changes.

Hustler's Funk

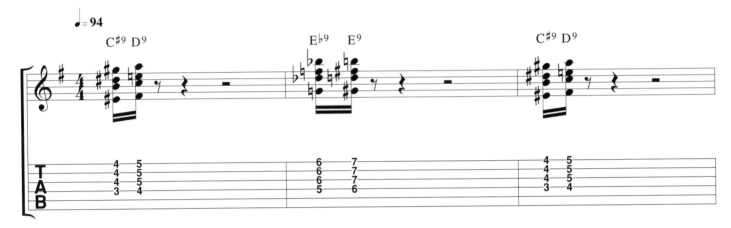

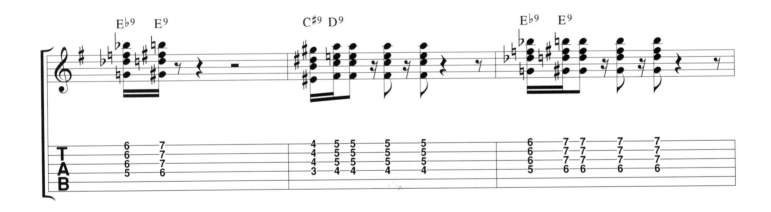

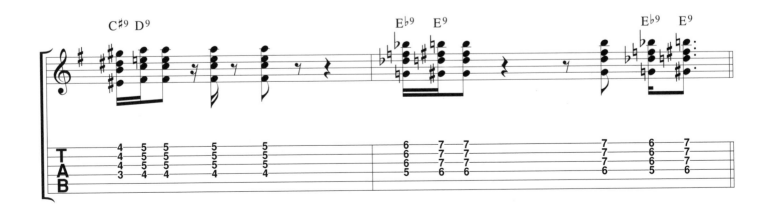

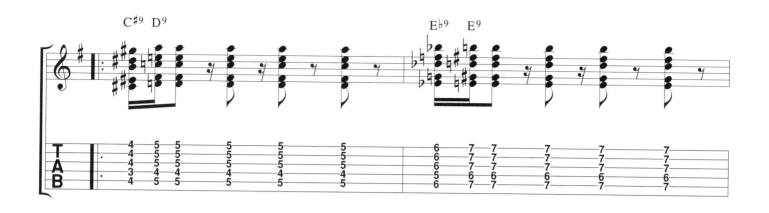

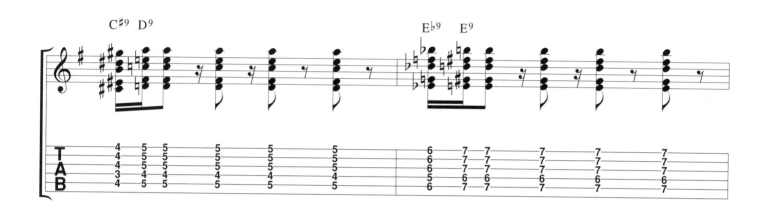

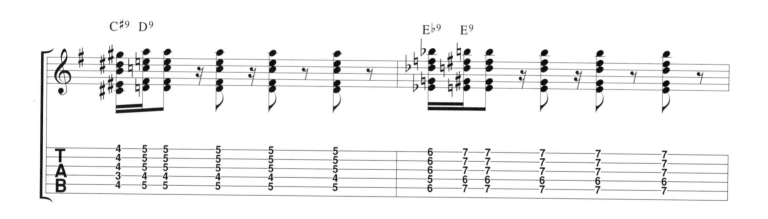

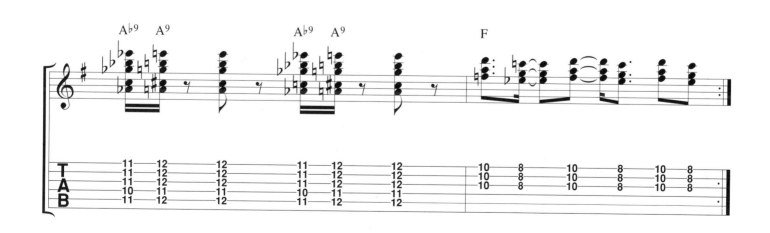

39

Funk Intro

Poor Jamie. You can guess the script. *This* head-ache is the sort that probably can't be fixed with a couple of *Nurofen*! 'Jamie Gets A Headache' has a number of technical challenges for you. Funk often features quite extended runs of single notes where the guitar is doubling a bass or a keyboard or synth. Another feature is that some funk songs sometimes have a fancy start to lull you into a false sense of security before the killer riff comes

in. Here a tumbling run of 16th notes finally lands on an unexpected G7add13, but the main riff is on E. The main chord is E7♯9, commonly named the '**Hendrix**' chord because he used it in blues/rock numbers like 'Purple Haze'. But there's plenty of funk in **Jimi**'s later songs – just listen to 'Dolly Dagger' or 'Freedom'. The challenge is to play the chord then insert the short fills on beats 3 and 4 of the bar.

TRACKS 37+38

Jamie Gets A Headache

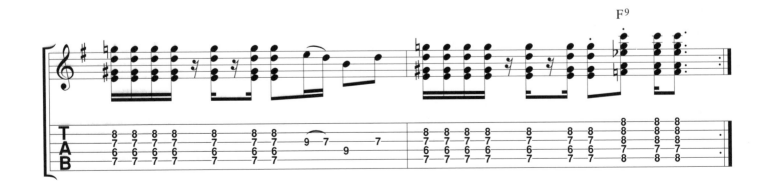

Accented Octaves

'Funk for the Good Guys' reverses the procedure.
This time you play a low single note riff and then
insert chords on the later beats of each bar.
Listen out for the accented octaves in bar 7.

Funk For The Good Guys

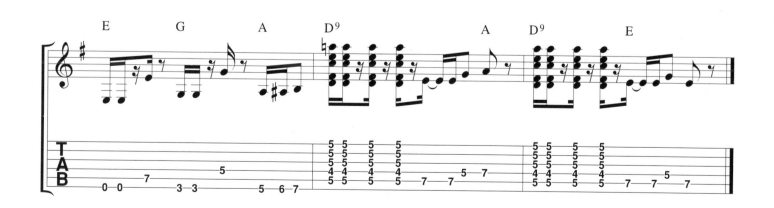

String Damping

When the guns come out people get *hoirt*... and there's 'Another Broken Heart'. Sometimes it's perfectly legitimate to use your thumb to hold down a bass string and damp a string at the same time. In this example the Cm7 shape in bar 1 needs a thumb on string 6 which will damp string 5. Your first finger barres the other notes. Your third finger is then free to add extra notes like the ones that crop up on the final beat of bars 1 and 2.

Another Broken Heart

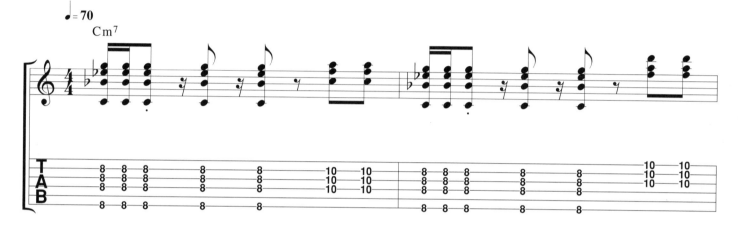

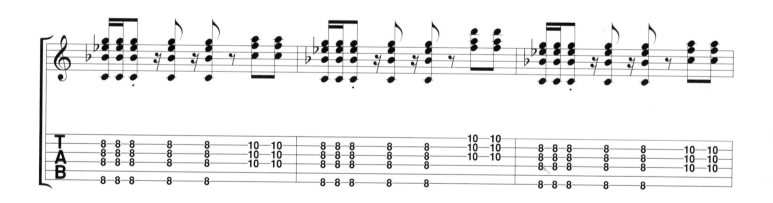

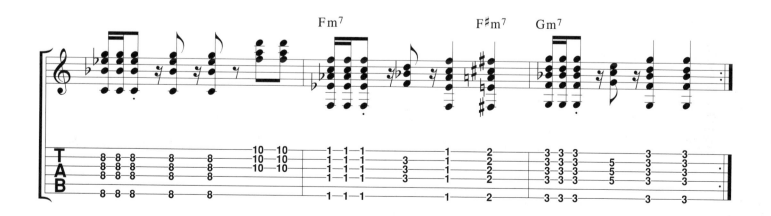

4: Classic Funky Grooves

Funk music came to prominence in the early
1970s. It developed out of a mixture of soul styles
and R'n'B in the 1960s. Chief among these styles
was that of the 'Godfather of Soul', **James
Brown**. **Brown**'s songs moved away from the
verse/chorus structures of mainstream soul and
replaced them with a more static music that was
highly rhythmic and pared back. 'Soul Shoes' is
an example of a **James Brown**-type groove,
using the little finger to push a fourth out from
the chord and up the neck a little.

TRACKS 43+44

Soul Shoes

'Scratch' Style

'Soul Heels' is another example of this type of groove, in the 'scratch' style of **Jimmy Nolan**. Each 'lick' consists of three chords on the same root note – at first Am7, A7add13 and A7.

In pieces like this the rhythm guitarist has to be absolutely in time and keep the groove going for however long is necessary, in order to get the hypnotic, repetitive effect.

TRACKS 45+46

Soul Heels

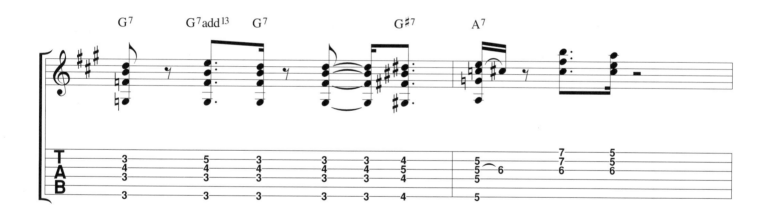

Chord Fills

'Soul Boots' takes this style one step further by incorporating fills between the chords. For the opening A7 chord use your thumb on the bass note. The hammer-on here changes the chord from a momentary Am7 to A7. The fills are mostly A pentatonic minor (A C D E G) until bars 14-16 when they become A pentatonic major (A B C♯ E F♯). The shift from minor to major changes the sound to a more upbeat feel. This track also has semi-tone shifting dominant 9ths.

TRACKS 47+48

Soul Boots

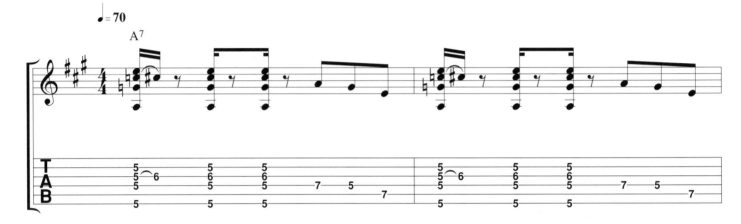

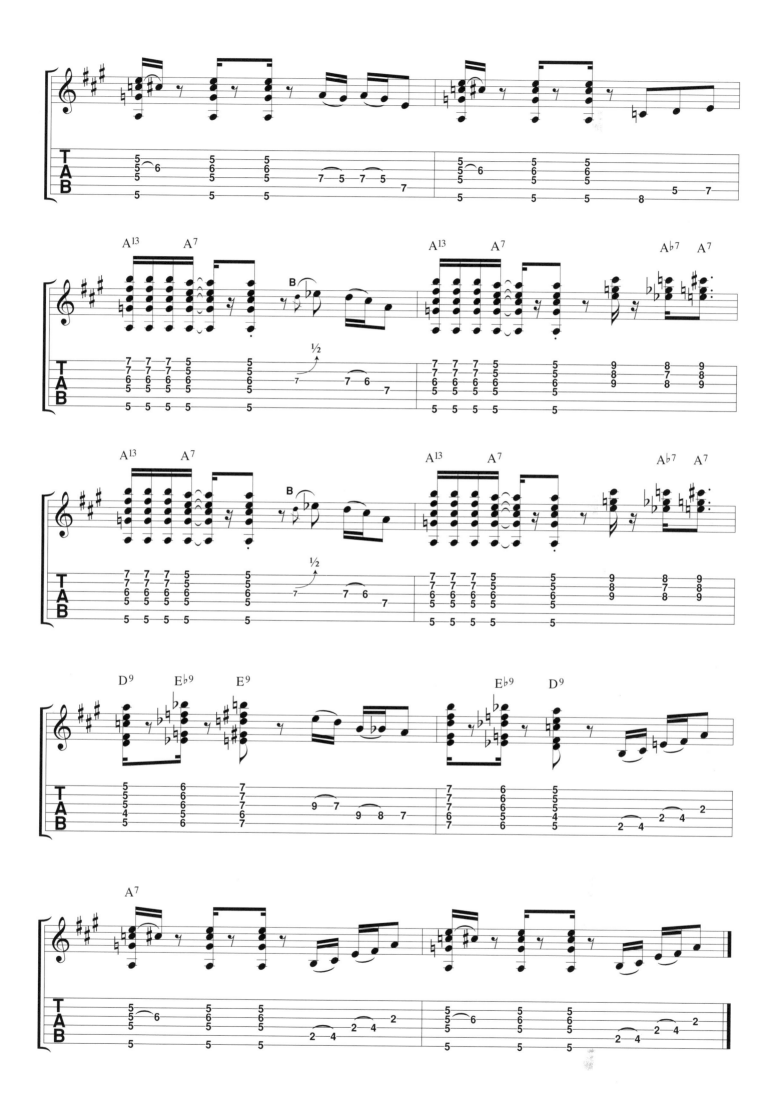

Hammer-Ons

'Miss Too Much' is another example of using the thumb to hold down the bass string and damp the 5th. The fills in bar 2 and 4 are created by using barres and hammering on low notes.

This style is associated with **Hendrix**, although he actually learned it from pre-psychedelic soul music. Take things nice and smooth for this track.

 **TRACKS 49+50**

Miss Too Much

►► *THE GAP BAND*

More Fills

'Chester's Shuffle' also uses the 'bass string thumb technique', with a combined hammer-on and a creeping semi-tone shift that gives a nice funk riff. Notice how the fills can be squeezed in at the end of the bars.

TRACKS 51+52

Chester's Shuffle

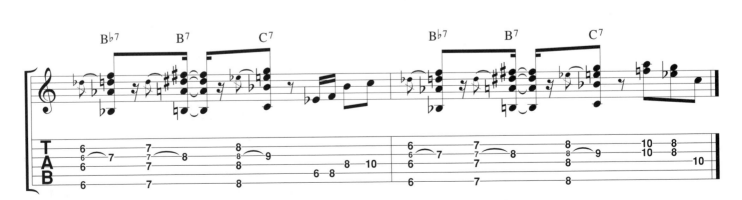

Classic Funk Rhythm

Now for a classic soul/funk rhythm idea. Take a minor 7 chord shape and play around with lifting the second and third fingers off and putting them back on. This can be done quite fast with a continuous 16th note damped strum if you want to. 'Deep Midnight' also has semi-tone shifts in the chords, and listen for the expressive minor 9 towards the end.

TRACKS 53+54

Deep Midnight

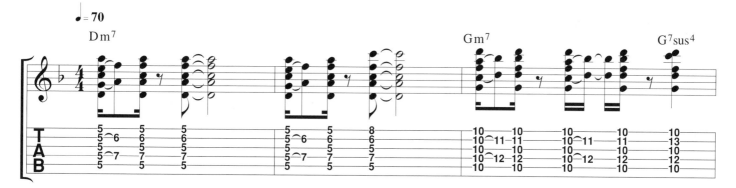

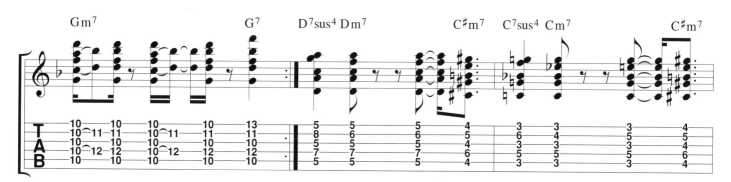

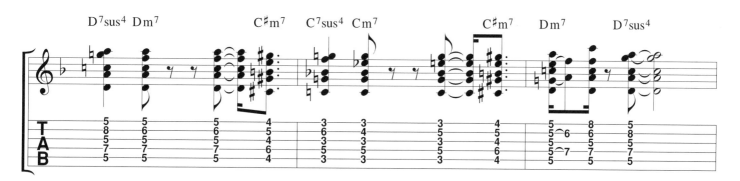

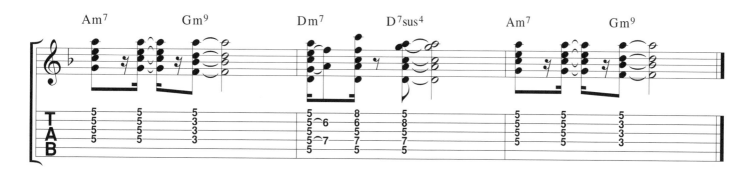

D Natural Minor Fills

Now let's take this minor 7 riff idea, slow it down, and put in some fills. The fills in 'Slow Midnight' are based on the scale of D natural minor (D E F G A B♭ C). You can find many variants on this. Notice the exotic-sounding fourths in bar 5.

 **TRACKS 55+56**

Slow Midnight

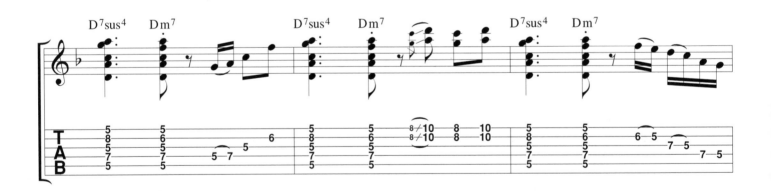

Clipped Chords

When it comes to '60s soul, bands didn't get much funkier than the legendary **Booker T. And the MGs**. Here's a soul groove such as they might have used on a **Wilson Pickett** or **Otis Redding** song. 'Funky Vintage' starts with some block chords before settling down into a three-chord riff where the rhythm guitar's job is to nail the off-beat with clipped chords. On the G to E part watch out for the little lead fills that **Steve Cropper** would often put in between the changes.

Funky Vintage

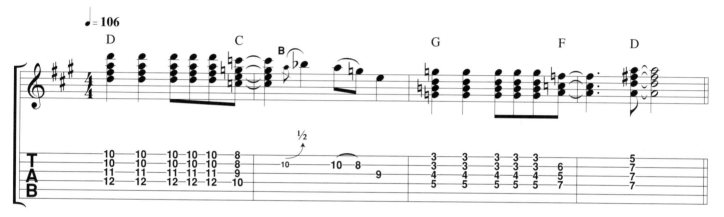

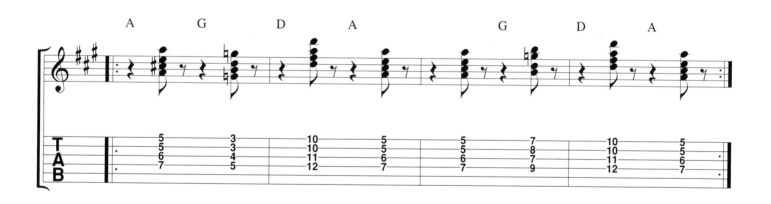

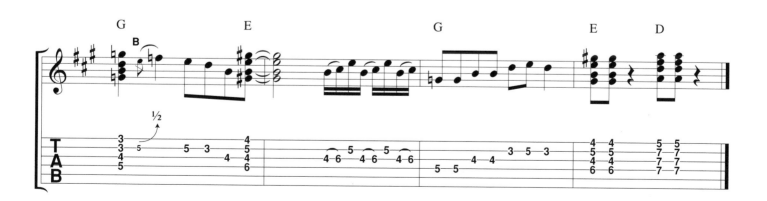

Sixths And Thirds

'Funky Vintage No. 2' features a different approach to the same sequence. This is what a decorative guitar part might be doing. On the intro we have a run of sixths with their distinctive 'hollow' sound, and then the 'closed' but sweet sound of thirds. The G-E change is played first as sixths, then as thirds, so you can hear how they sound over the same change. When you play consecutive sixths make sure that the lower note is played by the second finger, with the top note taken either by the first or the third. This helps to make them smooth.

TRACKS 59+60

Funky Vintage No. 2

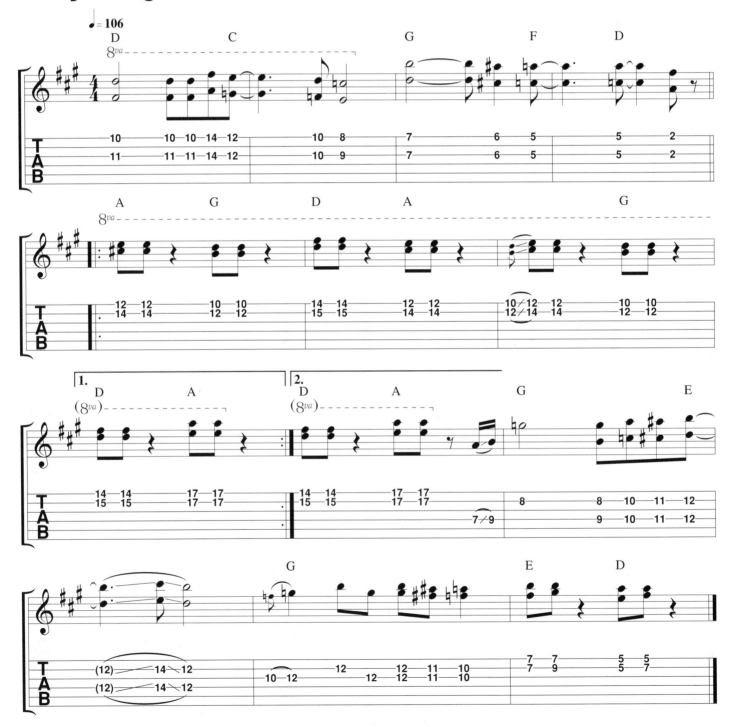

Soul Intro

Soul numbers on the **Atlantic** or **Stax** labels sometimes had dramatic intros which were great vehicles for live performance. 'When the Job's Done' demonstrates one of these, with full chords, fills, and even a bar of 2/4, before the build-up into the main verse groove.

This features a root note, a chord and a fill in each bar, and is an interesting way of getting out of the limitation of simply playing a chord. Notice the expressive hammer-ons which recall **Steve Cropper**'s playing on a number like 'Sitting On The Dock Of The Bay'.

When The Job's Done

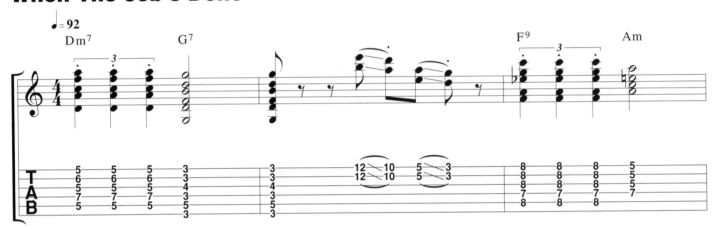

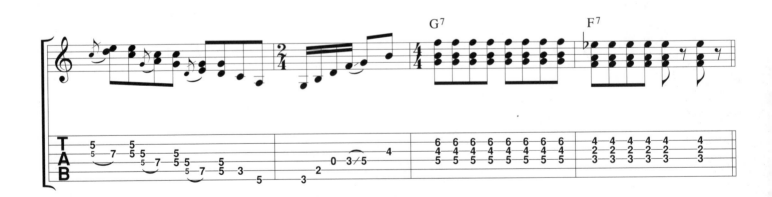

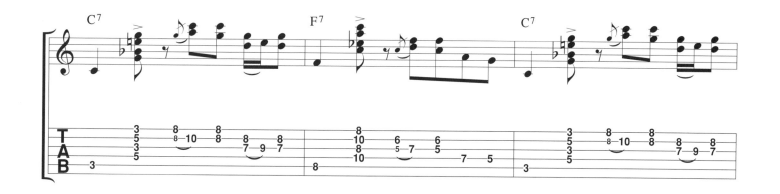

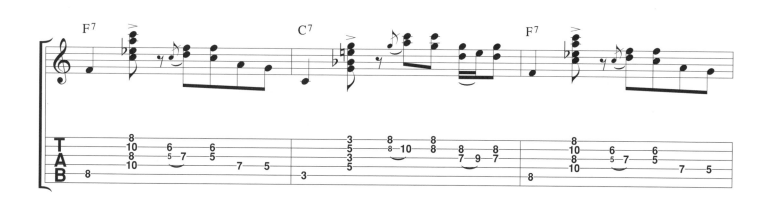

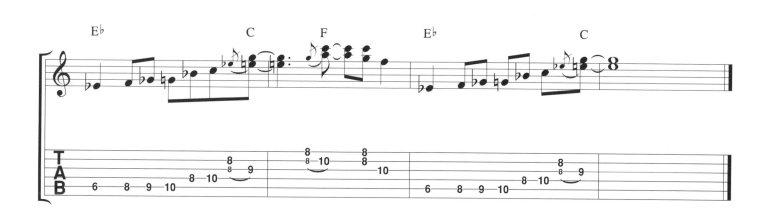

Motown Groove

No guide to funk and soul guitar would be complete without a homage to Motown – you can't forget the Motorcity! Some of the Motown records feature up to three guitar parts at once. On 'Can't Hurry Love,' for example, you will hear slashed high-pitched downbeat guitar chords such as you played on track 2. So 'Aurora'

(yep, Chester got the girl in the end) uses the four string chords in a smooth, expressive rhythm such as might have been played by **Robert White**. To play this correctly you have to really caress the strings with your strumming hand, at the same time squeezing the chord shape on and off in the same rhythm.

TRACKS 63+64

Aurora

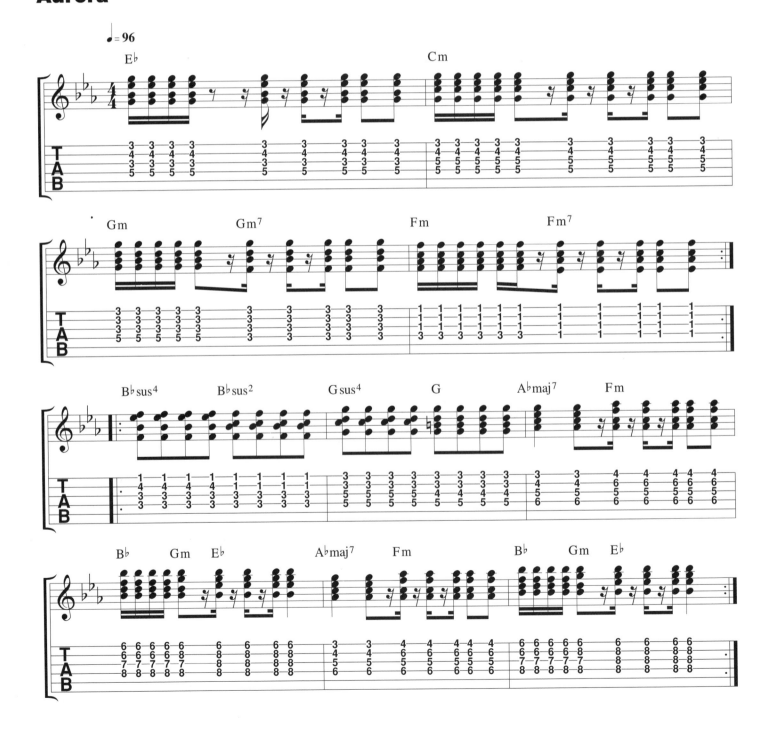

Motown Groove With Fills

'Aurora No. 2' is the same progression but with a delicate set of fills using two-note combinations (diads), hammer-ons, and thirds. This is the kind of guitar-playing you can hear on **Diana Ross**'s 'I'm Still Waiting'. It's a way of making a track more soulful through establishing an almost counter-melody on the guitar. Try to play it smooth and unhurried.

TRACKS 65+66

Aurora No. 2

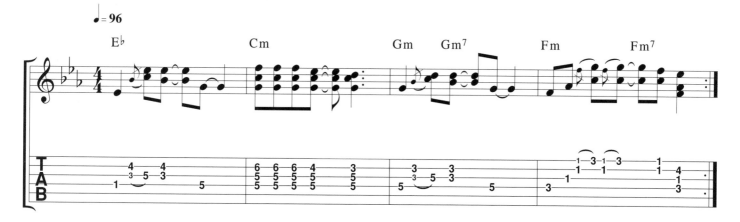

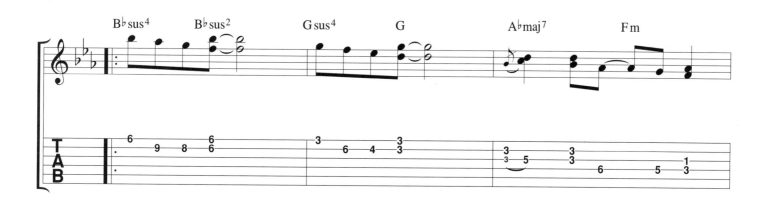

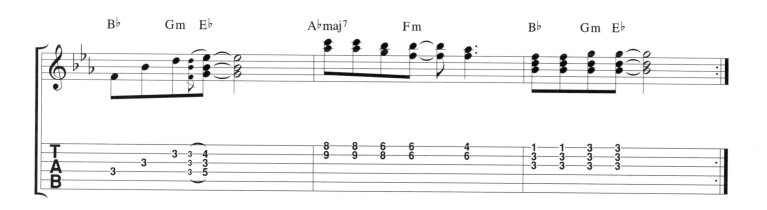

Funk Solo

Well, our hero has saved the day and walks into the distance of a city street. The credits are rolling and it's time to go home. I hope you have enjoyed this quick look at some of the guitar ideas that feature in funk and soul guitar. Most of what we have covered has been rhythmic, though we've looked at riffs and fills too. You might think, then, that maybe there aren't any guitar solos in funk. Of course, this isn't true. So let's finish with 'The Morning After', a lead solo you can get your teeth into... (not literally mind, unless you're a real Jimi nut!).

Hendrix was the clear influence for Ernie Isley's flamboyant, soaring lead on **The Isley Brothers'** 1970s hit 'That Lady' (check out 'House Burning Down'), and it's a tone that also features on the **Prince** song 'Purple Rain'. To get this guitar tone you need some distortion, phasing, and a little compression.

The solo starts with the scale of F♯ pentatonic minor (F♯ A B C♯ E) up around the 14th fret – a classic lead position. To make things more interesting (and challenging!) I've thrown in some unusual chord changes which require different scales to match. When you can play this solo you will realise why certain phrases fit over the chords in the second half of the piece. Till then, enjoy those bends!

TRACKS 67+68

The Morning After

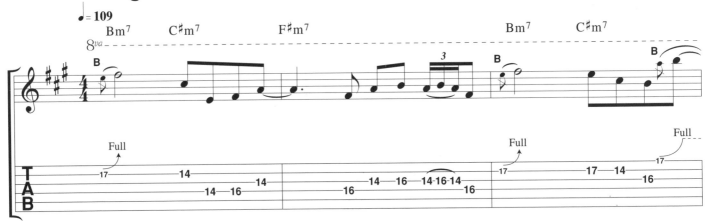

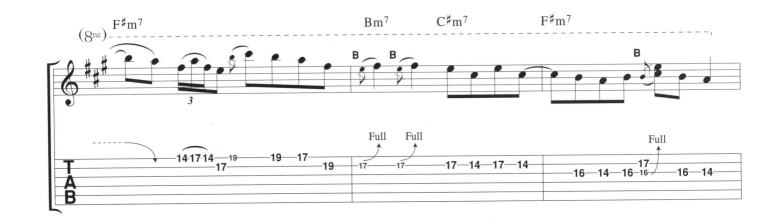

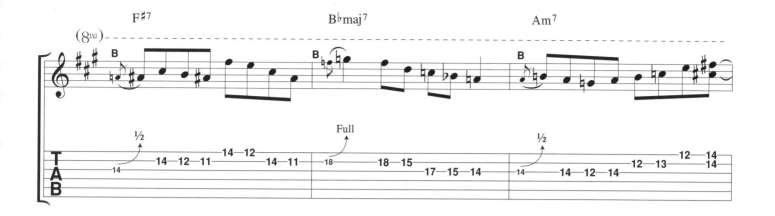

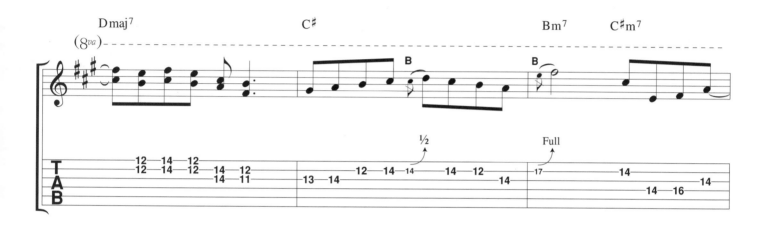

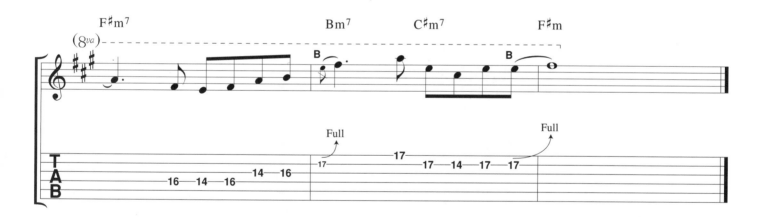

Discography

Here are some recommended key recordings by
some of the bands mentioned in this book:

The Average White Band	*Pickin' Up The Pieces: The Best Of Average White Band*
	1974-1980 (1992), AWB (1974)
Booker T. & the MG's	*The Very Best Of Booker T. & the MG's (1994*
	Green Onions (1962)
Bootsy Collins	*Stretchin' Out In Bootsy's Rubber Band (1976)*
	Back In The Day: The Best of Bootsy (1994)
Curtis Mayfield	*Curtis (1970), Superfly (1972)*
	The Anthology 1961-1977 (1992)
Earth, Wind & Fire	*Spirit (1976), The Best Of Earth, Wind & Fire, Vol.1 (1978)*
Funkadelic	*Maggot Brain (1971), One Nation Under a Groove (1978)*
George Clinton (solo)	*Computer Games (1982)*
Isley Brothers	*The Heat Is On (1975), The Isley Brothers Story, Vol.2 (1991)*
James Brown	*Foundations Of Funk: a Brand New Bag: 1964-1969 (1996),*
	Star Time (1991), Live At The Apollo (1963)
K.C. & the Sunshine Band	*The Best Of K.C. & The Sunshine Band (1990)*
Kool & The Gang	*Everything Is Kool & The Gang: Greatest Hits (1988),*
Parliament	*Mothership Connection (1977), Tear The Roof Off (1993),*
	The Best Of Parliament: Give Up The Funk (1995)
Sly & The Family Stone	*Stand! (1969), There's A Riot Goin' On (1971), Fresh (1973),*
	Anthology (1981)
The Commodores	*All The Greatest Hits (1982), Caught In The Act (1975)*
The Gap Band	*The Best Of The Gap Band (1995)*
The Ohio Players	*Ohio Players Gold (1976)*
Various Artists	*Motown Chart Busters Vol. 3 (1970) and Vol. 5 (1971)*

Further Reading

If you've enjoyed this book, why not check out some of the books shown below, available from all good music retailers or bookshops, or in case of difficulty, Music Sales Limited (see page 4). You can also visit our website: **www.musicsales.com**.

FastForward: Slide Guitar
AM958903

Learn how to use the bottleneck, altered tunings, string-damping and vibrato, and play in the style of Elmore James, Muddy Waters and Ry Cooder.

FastForward: Altered Guitar Tunings
AM958914

Discover the power of altered tunings to change your guitar sound. Improve your strumming, fingerpicking, rhythm guitar and bottleneck playing, in the styles of Joni Mitchell, Robert Johnson, James Taylor and Keith Richards.

FastForward: String Bending
AM958947

String bending is an essential technique for most popular styles of guitar music. This book will show you everything you need to know to play professional sounding riffs and solos used by all the famous players of blues, rock, folk and soul.

FastForward: Alternative Rock Guitar
AM958530

A complete history of alternative rock over the last four decades. Steer away from mainstream rock, and learn exactly what gave bands like Television, The Jam, The Smiths, The Stone Roses, R.E.M., U2, Nirvana and Radiohead their unique sounds.

Chord Chemistry
AM942580

We've all watched someone play and wondered 'What's that chord? It sounds great!' This book shows you how to create those great-sounding chords and sequences. Find out how to spice up basic repertoire, work on your strumming, and learn how to use 'add', 'sus', 7ths, 9ths and partial chords, and how to mix slash, root, pedal and barre chords into your sequences.

Chord Chemistry Songbook
AM952930

18 all-time great songs specially chosen to help you build your chord skills, including: 'Hey Joe', 'Happy Xmas (War Is Over)', 'Wonderwall', 'I Got You (I Feel Good)', and 'How Deep Is Your Love'.